Published in 2012 by Groundwood Books / House of Anansi Press
groundwoodbooks.com
Eighth printing 2021

Groundwood Books respectfully acknowledges that the land on which we
operate is the Traditional Territory of many Nations, including the Anishinabeg,
the Wendat and the Haudenosaunee. It is also the Treaty Lands of the
Mississaugas of the Credit.

We gratefully acknowledge the Government of Canada for their financial support
of our publishing program.

With the participation of the Government of Canada
Avec la participation du gouvernement du Canada | Canada

Library and Archives Canada Cataloguing in Publication
Serres, Alain
I have the right to be a child / author, Alain Serres; illustrator,
Aurélia Fronty ; translator, Helen Mixter.
Translation of: J'ai le droit d'être un enfant.
ISBN 978-1-55498-149-6
1. Children's rights — Juvenile literature.  2. Convention on the Rights of the
Child (1989) — Juvenile Literature.  I. Fronty, Aurélia
II. Mixter, Helen  III. Title.
HQ789.S4713 2012       j323.3'52       C2011-906895-8

The illustrations were done in acrylic on paper.
Printed and bound in South Korea

# I Have the Right to Be a Child

Alain Serres

Pictures by
Aurélia Fronty

Translated by
Helen Mixter

GROUNDWOOD BOOKS
HOUSE OF ANANSI PRESS
Toronto   Berkeley

I am a child

with eyes, hands,

a voice,

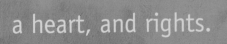

a heart, and rights.

I have the right
to a first name,
a last name,
a family that smiles at me,
and a country that I can call
my home.

I have the right
to have enough
food to eat and water to drink
so that I can grow.

My favorite thing is an orange.

You can eat it or drink its juice!

I have the right to live
under a roof,
to be warm

but not too hot,

not to be poor

and to have just enough

of what I need,

not more.

I have the right
to be cured
with the best
medicines
that were ever
invented.

And to run
and jump
and climb
and shout,

"It's so wonderful to feel good!"

I have the right
to go to school
without having to pay,
so that I can learn
how birds
or planes
or poppy seeds fly.

I have the same rights
whether I am a girl
or a boy.

Boys and girls love to sing
the same songs!

I have exactly the same right to be respected,

whether I am

black

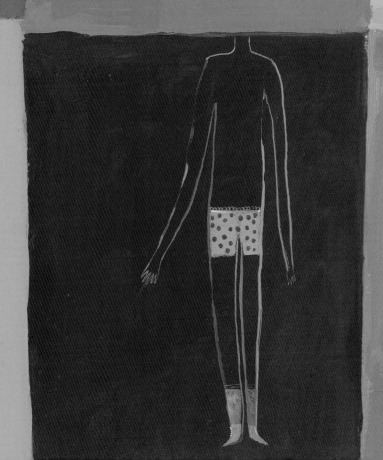

or white,

small or big,

rich or poor,

born here

or somewhere
else.

I have the right to be
helped by my parents,

my friends
and my country...

...if my body
doesn't work as well
as other children's.

I have the right to be free
from any kind of violence,
and no one has the right to
take advantage of me
because I am a child.
**No one.**

I have the right to go to school

and to refuse to go to work.

I'll choose a job when I've learned     everything I want to know!

I have the right to be
protected by adults

and to be sheltered from disasters under

a great big umbrella,
whether there's too much rain
or because of other sad things.

I have the right
never to experience
the storm of war
or the thunder of weapons.
I am afraid

of guided missiles
and smart bombs.

I have the right
to breathe clean air
that's as pure as the blue sky
or a newborn polar bear cub.

I have the right to play,
to create, to imagine,
to make faces
and to leap around...

...and also to have friends,
because dancing
alone
isn't very much fun.

I have the right to learn about friendship,
peace and respect for our planet
and for each human being
who lives on it,

for each animal
that inhabits it,
for each plant
that nourishes it.

I have the right
to express myself
completely freely —
to say what I truly think
about everything,

even if it doesn't always please my dad,
to say exactly how I feel,
even if it doesn't always please my mom.

I have the right to all these rights
just because I am a child,
especially if I live in one of the 193 states in the
world that have agreed to the Convention
on the Rights of the Child.*

When will
all children
everywhere
really have their
rights respected?

Tomorrow?
The day after tomorrow?
In twenty years?

*If I live
in one of
the very few
countries that
haven't agreed to
the Convention, like the
United States of America, then
I have the right to demand that my
country join! Should I not have the same
rights as every other child in the world?

We need our rights to be respected now — today — because it is right now — today — that we are children.

## THE UNITED NATIONS CONVENTION ON THE RIGHTS OF THE CHILD

In 1989 the leaders of countries belonging to the United Nations General Assembly adopted the Convention on the Rights of the Child, a special code of human rights for children under the age of eighteen. It recognizes that children require special protection since they are more vulnerable than adults. Children have rights as human beings. They are not the possessions of their parents, nor should they have to depend on charity for their needs.

All of the rights in the Convention are based on the following criteria: non-discrimination (the rights apply to *all* children), what is best for the child, the right to live and grow in good health, and the right for children to express their opinions in matters that concern them.

The Convention is made up of fifty-four articles, each describing a right that governments have a duty to honor and fulfill, as should everyone else. Very broadly they include the right to water, food, shelter, education and healthcare; the right to be protected from harm; the right to take an active part in family, community and cultural life; and the right to grow to one's fullest ability. All of these rights are equal — one is not more important than another. The Convention also establishes benchmarks for healthcare and schooling as well as legal and social aid. In 2000, two Optional Protocols were added — one designed to protect children from taking part in armed conflict, and the other to protect them from pornography, prostitution and the sale of children.

So far 196 states — including every member of the United Nations except the United States — are party to the Convention, having agreed to change or make laws and to develop practices and programs to support it. (The United States has signed to show their support for the Convention but has not yet ratified it. The United States has ratified the two Optional Protocols.) Each state that is party to the Convention must report regularly to the UN Committee on the Rights of the Child, which monitors whether or not the states are complying. UNICEF and other non-governmental organizations work in many countries to help achieve the Convention's goals.

Since the Convention came into being, there has been more awareness of children's rights the world over. But there is still a huge amount of work to do. Children continue to be threatened by war, poverty, disease, drought and discrimination because of their religion, ethnicity, or because they are girls. And even in wealthy countries like Canada and the United States there are still many children without the basic food, shelter and clean water that they need. Many lack sufficient education and healthcare, and live with abuse and neglect. Children's rights are of the greatest importance. We all have a duty to insist that they be observed.

To view the UN Convention on the Rights of the Child go to
https://www.ohchr.org/EN/ProfessionalInterest/Pages/CRC.aspx

States That Are Party to the UN Convention
on the Rights of the Child

| | | | | |
|---|---|---|---|---|
| Afghanistan | Congo | Holy See | Morocco | South Sudan |
| Albania | Cook Islands | Honduras | Mozambique | Spain |
| Algeria | Costa Rica | Hungary | Myanmar | Sri Lanka |
| Andorra | Côte d'Ivoire | Iceland | Namibia | St. Kitts and Nevis |
| Angola | Croatia | India | Nauru | St. Lucia |
| Antigua and Barbuda | Cuba | Indonesia | Nepal | St. Vincent and the |
| Argentina | Cyprus | Iran | Netherlands | Grenadines |
| Armenia | Czech Republic | Iraq | New Zealand | State of Palestine |
| Australia | Democratic People's | Ireland | Nicaragua | Sudan |
| Austria | Republic of Korea | Israel | Niger | Suriname |
| Azerbaijan | Democratic Republic of | Italy | Nigeria | Swaziland |
| Bahamas | the Congo | Jamaica | Niue | Sweden |
| Bahrain | Denmark | Japan | Norway | Switzerland |
| Bangladesh | Djibouti | Jordan | Oman | Syrian Arab Republic |
| Barbados | Dominica | Kazakhstan | Pakistan | Tajikistan |
| Belarus | Dominican Republic | Kenya | Palau | Thailand |
| Belgium | Ecuador | Kiribati | Panama | The former Yugoslav |
| Belize | Egypt | Kuwait | Papua New Guinea | Republic of |
| Benin | El Salvador | Kyrgyzstan | Paraguay | Macedonia |
| Bhutan | Equatorial Guinea | Lao People's Democratic | Peru | Timor-Leste |
| Bolivia | Eritrea | Republic | Philippines | Togo |
| Bosnia and Herzegovina | Estonia | Latvia | Poland | Tonga |
| Botswana | Ethiopia | Lebanon | Portugal | Trinidad and Tobago |
| Brazil | Fiji | Lesotho | Qatar | Tunisia |
| Brunei Darussalam | Finland | Liberia | Republic of Korea | Turkey |
| Bulgaria | France | Libya | Republic of Moldova | Turkmenistan |
| Burkina Faso | Gabon | Liechtenstein | Romania | Tuvalu |
| Burundi | Gambia | Lithuania | Russian Federation | Uganda |
| Cabo Verde | Georgia | Luxembourg | Rwanda | Ukraine |
| Cambodia | Germany | Madagascar | Samoa | United Arab Emirates |
| Cameroon | Ghana | Malawi | San Marino | United Kingdom of |
| Canada | Greece | Malaysia | São Tomé and Principe | Great Britain and |
| Central African Republic | Grenada | Maldives | Saudi Arabia | Northern Ireland |
| Chad | Guatemala | Mali | Senegal | United Republic of |
| Chile | Guinea | Malta | Serbia | Tanzania |
| China | Guinea-Bissau | Marshall Islands | Seychelles | Uruguay |
| Colombia | Guyana | Mauritania | Sierra Leone | Uzbekistan |
| Comoros | Haiti | Mauritius | Singapore | Vanuatu |
| | | Mexico | Slovakia | Venezuela |
| | | Micronesia | Slovenia | Viet Nam |
| | | Monaco | Solomon Islands | Yemen |
| | | Mongolia | Somalia | Zambia |
| | | Montenegro | South Africa | Zimbabwe |

## I Have the Right to Save My Planet

From the author and illustrator duo who created the award-winning *I Have the Right to Be a Child* and *I Have the Right to Culture* comes this beautifully illustrated picture book about a child's right to advocate for the environment they live in, as proclaimed in the Convention on the Rights of the Child.

Hardcover with jacket • ISBN 978-1-77306-487-1
EPUB • ISBN 978-1-77306-488-8

"A strong statement." — *Kirkus Reviews*

## I Have the Right to Culture

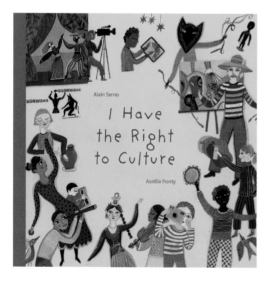

From the author and illustrator duo who created the award-winning *I Have the Right to Be a Child* and *I Have the Right to Save My Planet* comes this beautifully illustrated third book in the series. *I Have the Right to Culture* explores a child's right to be curious, and to experience all of humanity's shared knowledge, including music, art, dance and much more.

Hardcover with jacket • ISBN 978-1-77306-490-1
EPUB • ISBN 978-1-77306-491-8